My
Favorite
Horses

# PONIES

Stephanie Turnbull

A⁺
**Smart Apple Media**

Published by Smart Apple Media,
an imprint of Black Rabbit Books
P.O. Box 3263, Mankato, Minnesota, 56002
www.blackrabbitbooks.com

Designed by Hel James
Edited by Mary-Jane Wilkins

Cataloging-in-Publication Data is available from the Library of Congress

ISBN 978-1-62588-181-6

Photo acknowledgements
l = left, r = right, t = top, b = bottom
title page cynoclub; page 3 Eric Isselee; 4-5 Ainars Aunins;
6 Michele Goglio; 7 Olga_i; 8 Perry Correll; 9 Burry van den Brink;
10 marilyn barbone; 11 gorillaimages; 12 sy33; 13 EMJAY SMITH;
14 Alexandr Shevchenko; 15 SF photo; 17 pirita; 18 curtis; 19 Anastasija
Popova; 20 Nicky Rhodes; 21 Michael C. Gray; 22 Graeme Dawes;
23 Grant Glendinning. All images Shutterstock
Cover Zuzule/Shutterstock

Printed in China

DAD0055
032014
9 8 7 6 5 4 3 2 1

# Contents

# What are Ponies?

Ponies are small horses.

They have shorter legs, wider bodies, thicker necks, and broader heads than bigger horse breeds.

# Measuring Up

Horses are measured in hands from their feet to their withers (shoulders).

Horse breeds that are less than 14.2 hands high are usually called ponies.

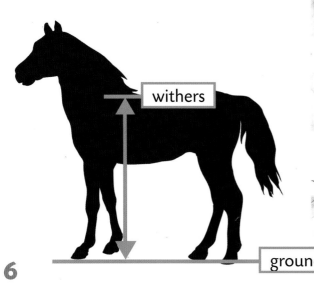

withers

ground

There is a huge difference between the biggest horses...

... and the smallest ponies!

# Horse or Pony?

Sometimes people call any horse a pony, even if it isn't a pony breed. For example, horses used for playing polo are always called ponies.

Polo ponies are slim, agile horses that are much taller than real ponies.

People may also confuse ponies with foals.

This foal is small like a pony, but it will grow into a large horse like its mother.

# Small and Smaller

The tallest ponies are sturdy
and muscular, like this
Welsh Mountain Pony…

… and the shortest are stout and stumpy, like this Shetland Pony.

# Outdoor Life

Many ponies come from cold, windswept places. They have thick coats and manes to help them keep warm.

Some ponies live in the wild all year around. They graze on grass and find streams to drink from.

# Tiny but Tough

Ponies may be small, but they're very strong. They often pull heavy carts or carriages that weigh far more than they do.

Some ponies are trained to
take part in driving events.

# Pony Riding

Ponies are the perfect first horses for young riders.

Well-trained ponies are gentle, friendly, and fun to ride.

There is a pony to suit everyone —no matter how small they are!

# Saddling Up

Many children join pony clubs to learn riding skills. They wear hard hats and padded trousers called jodhpurs.

First, new riders learn to sit properly and control their pony.

Later, they
may gallop
and jump.

# Fun and Games

Many skilled riders exercise their ponies on riding trails.

Ponies don't mind walking on rocky or hilly ground.

Some people ride or show
their ponies in competitions.
They may win prizes!

# Pony Care

Ponies must be kept clean and neat, with regular checks from a vet.

They eat less hay and grass than larger horses.

Ponies need lots of space to exercise. These young ponies love to run and play.

# Useful Words

**breed** A type of horse. Many small horse breeds are called ponies.

**foal** A horse or pony that is less than a year old.

**gallop** The fastest way a horse can run, lifting all four hooves off the ground.

**hand** A unit of measurement for the height of horses.

# Index